Look at My Neighborhood

by Barbara L. Luciano
illustrated by Michael Rex

Scott Foresman
is an imprint of

Glenview, Illinois • Boston, Massachusetts • Chandler, Arizona
Upper Saddle River, New Jersey

Every effort has been made to secure permission and provide appropriate credit for photographic material. The publisher deeply regrets any omission and pledges to correct errors called to its attention in subsequent editions.

Unless otherwise acknowledged, all photographs are the property of Scott Foresman, a division of Pearson Education.

Illustrations by Michael Rex

ISBN 13: 978-0-328-50730-6
ISBN 10:   0-328-50730-X

10 V010 15 14 13

I live in a city.

Look at my neighborhood.

Lots of people live and work here.

I live in the country.

Look at my neighborhood.

Many farm animals live here.

I live in a city.

Look at my neighborhood.

I have pals who pitch and catch.

I live in a town.

Look at my neighborhood.

I ride my bike with Chad.

I live at a lake.

Look at my neighborhood.

I swim and go out in boats.

You saw many neighborhoods.

They are not the same.

Which one is like yours?